P9-ARG-284

My Country
France

Annabelle Lynch

Smart Apple Media

Published by Smart Apple Media
P.O. Box 3263, Mankato, Minnesota 56002
www.blackrabbitbooks.com

Published by arrangement with the Watts Publishing
Group LTD, London.

Library of Congress Cataloging-in-Publication Data

Lynch, Annabelle.
France / Annabelle Lynch
p. cm.—(My country)
Summary: "Describes France's landscape, weather, and
things to see in France. Readers meet Camille, who tells
about France's school, food, and family. Includes a fact
page with information on the geography of France, as well
as its population and religion"—Provided by publisher.
Includes bibliographical references and index.
ISBN 978-1-59920-905-0 (library binding)
1. France—Juvenile literature. I. Title.
DC17.B54 2015~
944—dc23

      2012024749

Series Editor: Paul Rockett
Series Designer: Paul Cherrill for Basement68
Picture Researcher: Diana Morris

Every attempt has been made to clear copyright. Should
there be any inadvertent omission please apply to the
publisher for rectification.

Picture credits: auremar/Shutterstock: 13t; Marta
Benavides/istockphoto: front cover cl; Kevin Calvin/Alamy:
12; Alexander Chaikin/Shutterstock: 7t; Tor Eigeland/Alamy:
front cover c, 4, 13b, 16b, 22; Fretschi/Shutterstock: 20b;
Robert Fried/Alamy: 15; Botond Horvath/Shutterstock: 9;
Pierre Jacques/Hemis/Alamy: 11; JeniFoto/Shutterstock:
5; Robert Linton/istockphoto: 13c; Maugli/Shutterstock:
1, 21; Phillip Minnis /Shutterstock: 20t; mountainpix /
Shutterstock: 3, 17t; Luba V Nel/Shutterstock: 19; PHB.
cz Richard Semik/Shutterstock: 7b; Photononstop/
Superstock: 10; Radius/Superstock: 14; Ray Roberts/
Alamy: 16c; Samot/Shutterstock: 2, 8; Paul Tavener/Alamy:
18; Paul Villecourt/Watts: 6; witchcraft/Shutterstock:
front cover cr; Stephan Zabel/istockphoto: 17b.

Printed in Stevens Point, Wisconsin at Worzalla
PO 1654
4-2014

9 8 7 6 5 4 3 2 1

Contents

All words in **bold**
appear in the
glossary on page 23.

France in the World

> *Bonjour!* My name is Camille and I come from France.

France's place in the world

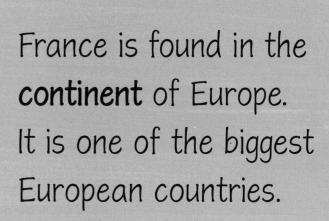

France is found in the **continent** of Europe. It is one of the biggest European countries.

Strasbourg has many old buildings.

I live in the city of Strasbourg. Strasbourg is the **capital** of a region called Alsace.

People Who Live in France

Around 65 million people live in France today. Over the years, people from all over the world have come to live here.

My classmates have family from Italy, Asia, and Africa.

Most people in France live in or near big cities, such as Paris and Marseille, where there are lots of jobs. Fewer people live in the country.

This is Paris, the capital city of France.

My aunt and cousin live in the country and have a pet donkey!

What France Looks Like

France's **landscape** changes from place to place. There are big cities, but there are also green forests and high mountains.

Around France, there are lots of **vineyards** where grapes are grown.

In eastern France, you can find snowy mountains. Along the south and west **coasts** there are long, sandy beaches where people go to swim, surf, and have fun!

This is Biarritz, where we go surfing on our vacations.

At Home with My Family

If the weather is nice we eat outside.

Family life is important in France. Most families eat together every evening and on weekends. Meals can go on for a long time.

On weekends and on special days, we often get together with grandparents, aunts, uncles, and cousins.

Here we are celebrating my aunt's birthday.

What We Eat

French people love good food! France makes some of the best cheese, bread, and wine in the world.

We eat long loaves of bread called baguettes with most meals.

Favorite French snacks include croissants or crêpes (pancakes). For a main meal, we often eat cassoulet, which is a type of **stew** with beans, sausage, and duck.

what would you put on this crêpe?

we eat bread with cassoulet to mop up all the sauce.

I eat croissants for breakfast. What do you have?

13

Going to School

In France, we start school at 6 years old at an *école primaire*. I go to an *école primaire*. When you are 11, you move on to a *collège*. From 15 to 18, you go to a different school called a *lycée*.

This is my brother on the steps of his new school.

We have a long lunch every day, and lots of people go home to eat. At many schools, we have free time every Wednesday afternoon to play sports or enjoy music.

Soccer is the most popular sport in France.

 # Having Fun

When we're not at school or work, we have fun! Lots of people spend time outside playing. At home, we watch TV and play games such as ping-pong.

A lot of people enjoy bicycling around France.

I love going to the pool with my friends in the summer. What do you like doing?

During the summer, lots of French people go camping or head to the beach. In winter, they go to the mountains where they can ski, skate, or **snowboard**.

The French Alps are a great place to go snowboarding.

We go camping every year. It's fun!

Festivals and Celebrations

There are **festivals** throughout the year in France. On July 14th, we celebrate Bastille Day to remember the beginning of the **French Revolution** in 1789.

On Bastille Day, there are lots of parties and fireworks.

Around France, there are smaller festivals. These often celebrate things that are special to a place, such as **local** foods, or remember something that happened there.

In Menton, in the south of France, they have a festival to celebrate the growing of lemons.

Things to See

France has wonderful places to visit! In Paris, you can climb the famous Eiffel Tower and look out over the city. You can also enjoy a boat ride on the Seine River.

The Eiffel Tower is one of the most recognizable buildings in the world!

Traveling on the Seine River is a great way to see Paris.

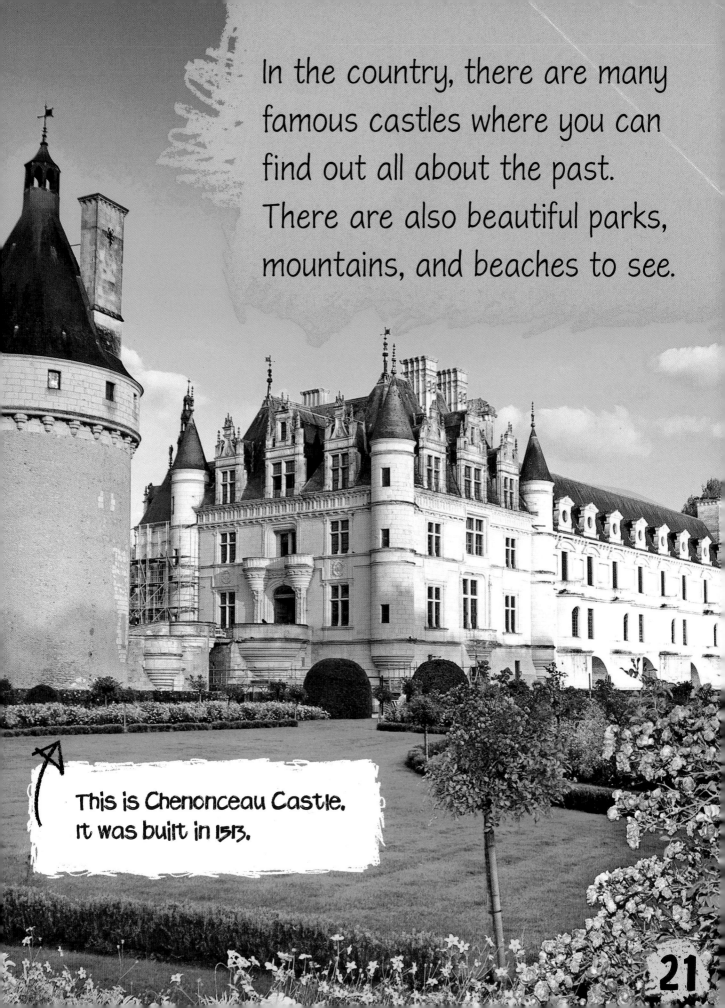

In the country, there are many famous castles where you can find out all about the past. There are also beautiful parks, mountains, and beaches to see.

This is Chenonceau Castle. It was built in 1513.

Here are some facts about my country!

Fast Facts about France

Capital city = Paris

Population = 65,312,249

Area = 211,210 square miles
  (547,030 km²)

Language = French

National holiday = July 14 (Bastille Day)

Currency = the euro

Main religions = Christian, Muslim, Jewish

Longest river = Loire River, 629 miles (1,012 km)

Highest mountain = Mont Blanc, 15,780 feet (4,810 m)

Glossary

capital the most important city in a country

coast where the land meets the sea

continent one of the seven main areas of land in the world

festival a special time when people celebrate something

French Revolution when the people of France came together in 1789 to change how the country was run

landscape what a place or area looks like

local belonging to a particular place

snowboard to slide down a snowy slope on a special board

stew a meal, usually made of meat and vegetables, that is cooked slowly

vineyard an area where grapes are grown to make wine

Further Information

Websites

http://www.chiddingstone.kent.sch.uk/homework/france.html

http://www.kids-world-travel-guide.com/france-facts.html

http://kids.nationalgeographic.com/kids/places/find/france/

Books

Brooks, Susie. *Let's Visit France.* PowerKids Press, 2010

Savery, Annabel. *France (Been There).* Smart Apple Media, 2012

Index